BRITAIN IN OLD ~~~~~~~~~~PHS

BLACKBURN

M A R T I N   B A G G O L E Y

SUTTON PUBLISHING LIMITED

Sutton Publishing Limited
Phoenix Mill · Thrupp · Stroud
Gloucestershire · GL5 2BU

First published 1996

Reprinted in 2002 (twice), 2004

Copyright © Martin Baggoley, 1996

British Library Cataloguing in Publication Data
A catalogue record for this book is available from the
British Library.

ISBN 0-7509-1262-6

Typeset in 10/12 Perpetua.
Typesetting and origination by
Sutton Publishing Limited.
Printed in Great Britain by
J.H. Haynes & Co. Ltd, Sparkford.

Title page: the Blackburn Olympic FA Cup winning team of 1883 who beat Old Etonians by two goals to one at the Oval. They became the first Lancashire team to win the famous trophy, thanks to scorers Costley and Matthews.

This late Victorian photograph is of Wilpshire, to the north of Blackburn town centre. This suburb was popular with the more well-off folk, and on the left is the Wilpshire Hotel, which is still standing today.

CONTENTS

INTRODUCTION

To many, Blackburn is the archetypal Lancashire cotton town of cobbled streets and mill chimneys. Its history, however, can be traced back many centuries. In Norman times a settlement first grew there, which took its name from the river on which it stood, becoming known as Blake Burn. It developed into an important administrative area and Blackburn became one of Lancashire's hundreds, so significant in early local government. It also became commercially important to the region with a weekly market being held there, along with annual fairs at Easter, in May and in October.

Textiles have long been important to Blackburn's growth and by the late eighteenth century, the town was renowned for its calicos. One visitor at that time commented on how the fields which surrounded the town were white with the materials lying out to bleach in the sun.

In 1801 the town's population reached 11,980 and the weavers employed locally worked at home, where they kept their looms. In 1901 the population had grown to 129,210 and the massive expansion of the cotton industry meant that more than 100 mills were built during that period.

Blackburn had clearly experienced a profound transformation, based purely on cotton. The opening of the Leeds and Liverpool Canal early in the nineteenth century, also made the transportation of goods much easier and this economic expansion was given a further boost in mid-century, with the opening of the railway network.

As Blackburn prospered, the townsfolk petitioned the Queen for a Charter of Incorporation and in 1851 the town council met for the first time, in the Old Sessions House in Heaton Street, to elect the first mayor and other corporation officials. The following fifty years witnessed the construction of many public buildings and leisure facilities which included an infirmary, town hall, workhouse and technical college; Corporation Park opened, together with a library and public baths. These buildings and facilities reflected the growing importance of the town, and offered its inhabitants new leisure opportunities.

Pride in the town and its economic achievements found expression in the support given to its leading football clubs. During the 1870s and 1880s the professional sides of the north of England, particularly those in the cotton towns of East Lancashire such as Darwen and Blackburn, challenged the supremacy of the amateur sides of the south, centred mainly on public schools, universities and the army. Blackburn Olympic became the first northern team to win the FA Cup in 1883, but the competition was dominated by rivals Blackburn Rovers for the next decade. Between 1882 and 1891 a Blackburn team was involved in no less than seven finals and in 1888 Blackburn Rovers became one of the original members of the Football League.

Despite the importance of cotton, there have of course been other industries associated with Blackburn. One of the most notable has been brewing and several breweries have played an integral part in the town's history. There have also been trades more directly associated with cotton, such as the manufacture of shuttles. It is a tribute to Blackburn folk that although there has been a great decline in the cotton trade during the past century, they have always been able to adapt and turn their skills to service industries, engineering and other manufacturing concerns.

The photographs in this book mainly cover the period between the mid-nineteenth and mid-twentieth centuries. They show the mills, factories, churches, schools, parks, cinemas and pubs which have been such an important part of Blackburn's past. Also included are photographs of the people who have lived and worked there or served the town, from millhands to mayors and Members of Parliament, each of whom, in his or her own way, has contributed to Blackburn's story.

Martin Baggoley
1996

STREET SCENES & VIEWS

This panoramic view of Blackburn was taken in 1880 from a high point in Corporation Park, and many of the town's mill chimneys can be seen rising from the mass of streets. In the foreground are the Russian cannon, trophies of the Crimean War, which were removed in August 1940 to be turned into scrap metal to help the war effort.

The cathedral dominates this aerial view of the town centre, taken in the early 1930s. The Boulevard can be seen to the right, with Jubilee Street running along the bottom. Darwen Street leads off it and up to the market-place. The River Blakewater is in the top centre of the photograph.

A policeman stands where Church Street, King William Street and Darwen Street converged in 1954. This is where the market cross was located until it mysteriously disappeared in the early nineteenth century.

The Market Tower and Hall provide the backdrop to this Edwardian view of the market-place. The area was redeveloped and the Tower subsequently demolished on 30 December 1964.

There was room for almost 300 stalls at the outdoor market and in this 1906 scene a young woman rather self-consciously buys some produce.

Victoria Street, seen here at about the same time, overlooked the outdoor market. Slaters, the shop on the corner, was a grocer, and a few doors further down were the Maypole Dairy Company and Abraham Altham Ltd, a tea merchant.

To the right of this 1898 view of Church Street, by then an important commercial area, are the offices of the Wigan Coal and Iron Company. They operated a fleet of seventy boats on the Leeds–Liverpool Canal, supplying coal to Lancashire's industries.

Further down Church Street was the brush manufacturer, Pickering, founded in 1825. On display in their window were the many different types of brush they made, although they were especially renowned for their strong brooms used in stables.

Prominent in this Victorian view of Darwen Street are the premises of Poldings, a corn merchants founded in 1802. Their eight spacious storerooms held cornflour, beans, peas and cereals. The general post office was later built on this site.

This other view of Darwen Street shows the impressive Merchants Hotel, on the corner of Jubilee Street.

Built in 1816, these splendid Georgian houses were popular with the local gentry. By the time of this 1929 photograph, the house on the corner of Old Bank Street was a Salvation Army Hostel.

Although a little dilapidated by 1958, this courtyard at the rear of King Street is a reminder of grander days – it was here that the stables were located. At one time James Brogden, gentleman, and the parish clerk James Radcliffe lived in the two houses seen here.

King William Street in 1922 was clearly a major thoroughfare, and there was something of a cavalier attitude towards parking.

Blakey Moor in the 1920s, with the Public Halls on the right, which had been completed in 1921, and the Technical College in the background. The town's old cattle market used to be held on Blakey Moor.

A cobbled St Peter's Street photographed in the 1890s. The headquarters of George Briggs and Sons, a firm of tanners, curriers and leather merchants are in the background.

Shorrock Fold, seen here in 1960, was an old right of way leading through Haworth Square towards the Tacketts. There were two inns in the Fold, The Star, which was also used as a lock up, and The Black Lion. The house on the right used to belong to the sexton of the parish church.

These weavers' cottages in Winter Street were some of Blackburn's oldest properties and dated back to the early eighteenth century. Built before the massive growth of mills, each had a separate handloom shop attached.

These handloom weavers' cottages were built in about 1800, when it was still usual for weavers to work at home. The local poet, John Pickup, was born on this row in Cleaver Street in 1860.

Syke Street takes its name from the local term 'syke', meaning a tunnel draining into the River Blakewater. The houses were built in the early nineteenth century and the cellars, the steps down to which can be seen in this 1958 view, were also used as dwellings.

Suddell Cross seen here in 1953, decorated for the coronation celebrations, was once the site of an enormous gas lamp. This was destroyed by a gas explosion in 1882, in which one man was killed.

Of interest in this 1910 scene of the Salford district, near to the junction with Railway Road, is the difference in the two shop fronts. To the left is the façade of Boyle's House Furnishers and the old-fashioned window shows that this shop is still in the original form. In contrast, the taller building to the right, which is the premises of saddlers Leeming and Yates, has been renovated in the more modern style.

Salford Bridge in 1952, before the culvert was built when the area was redeveloped. It shows the River Blakewater which in 1804, owing to dry weather and pollution from the rinsings of local dyehouses, had become a stagnant ditch. Raw sewage was being put straight into the river right up until the 1860s.

Union Street Bridge, *c.* 1952.

Salford's deterioration led to massive improvements in the 1880s, when this photograph was taken. It shows the former Railway Road premises of the chemists Pickup and Co., and Wordens which was a tobacconist and hairdressers. Both firms relocated to Penney Street.

The great expansion of the railways during the nineteenth century resulted in many fine examples of railway architecture. This is the Feniscowles Viaduct, built for the Blackburn to Chorley line.

Witton Stocks, seen here in the early twentieth century, was so named as it was here that the local stocks were located. It became a popular place of residence for the more well-to-do townsfolk and expanded greatly throughout the nineteenth century.

Preston New Road, pictured in 1910, was popular with local mill owners and senior employees. The houses thus became the targets for rioting mill workers in May 1878. All the houses had to be boarded up against missiles and a detachment of infantry was sent to disperse a stone-throwing mob.

Whalley New Road, to the north of the town centre, was built by a turnpike trust in 1820, to provide an improved route out of the town. The houses along it were both spacious and comfortable.

New Bank Road, to the west of the town, also provided superior types of houses for Blackburn's wealthier residents.

This small shop and other buildings on the corner of Limbrick and Kirkham Lane, seen in about 1900, illustrates how early Blackburn had developed in a rather haphazard manner – without much planning.

The town centre was largely redeveloped by the 1970s, with many well-known landmarks disappearing. The functional new arcade made shopping that much easier, but a great deal of the town's character had also gone.

Allotments were of great importance to working men as a leisure pursuit; they provided a break from the tedium of the mill and factory routine. At times of need, they were also important in supplementing the family's provisions. This splendid view is of the council allotments at Feniscliffe, with the railway line to the left, the canal to the right, and the town towards the top of the photograph.

THE LAKE,
CORPORATION PARK,

Corporation Park was opened on 22 October 1857 by the mayor William Pilkington, on land purchased from Joseph Fielden, Lord of the Manor, for £3,237 6s 3d. The land contained two natural lakes, The Can and Big Can, shown in this photograph, which had been Blackburn's earliest reservoirs. During the cotton famine in the 1860s, hundreds of laid-off mill workers were employed in improving the park. In the 1920s the park's facilities were greatly enhanced with the building of two bowling greens, five tennis courts, a pavilion and a terraced walk.

A ladies' doubles match in progress on a Corporation Park tennis court in the summer of 1923. Tennis was considered suitable for young ladies, as they could wear long skirts while playing.

There was seating for almost 2,000 spectators at the park's bandstand which opened on 17 September 1909. At the opening ceremony the band of the 2nd Battalion Border Regiment played throughout the afternoon and evening.

Queen's Park was laid out in 1887 at a cost of £10,000 and became a popular place of recreation for Blackburn folk. This 1917 postcard shows one of the park's two circular bowling greens.

Just over three of Queen's Park's thirty-three acres were taken up by a large boating lake, seen here in 1922, with the boathouse in the background.

To commemorate the royal visit to Blackburn in July 1913, cotton manufacturers Duckworth and Eddleston donated seventeen acres of land at Roe Green to create a public park. These plans were delayed because of the First World War and it was not until 1923 that Roe Lee Park was built as part of a housing scheme for 302 homes.

Witton Park was formerly the estate of the Fielden family and this tranquil scene taken in the 1950s is of the River Darwen, which flowed through the estate.

BUILDINGS

The former calendar house on Old Chapel Street was purchased by Blackburn's Methodists in about 1780 and converted into the town's original Wesleyan Chapel. John Wesley preached there several times and on Sunday 18 April 1784 he noted that, despite a large congregation, there was 'not one well-dressed person among them'. From 1786 it was used for commercial purposes and when this photograph was taken in the 1920s, it was being used by a builder and a rag merchant.

This run-down building, photographed in 1959, is the Sessions House on Heaton Street. Built in 1804 all of the town's important meetings were held here, including that on 28 November 1850 when the original petition to the Queen for a Charter of Incorporation was drawn up. Local landowners and ratepayers believed that the Blackburn Improvement Commissioners, who then governed the town were inadequate, given the town's growth. The Charter was granted and on 28 August 1851 the first Mayor, William Henry Hornby, was elected, together with twelve aldermen and thirty-six councillors.

The town hall, built in the classic style and situated on the north side of the market-place, was opened on 30 October 1856 by the mayor William Hoole. This photograph was taken in 1951, during the town's centenary celebrations.

On the ground floor of the town hall was the mayor's parlour. This 1927 photograph reveals a formal but nevertheless attractive room.

The handsome council chamber occupied much of the upper storey of the town hall and some idea of its grandeur can be gained from this photograph taken in the 1930s, showing a council meeting in progress.

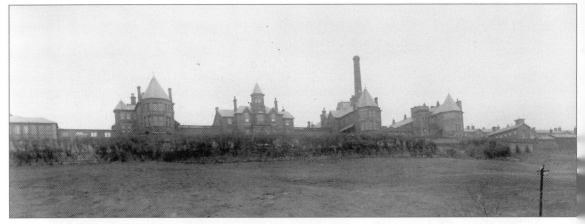

The Blackburn Poor Law Union was formed in 1836 and the Board of Guardians met for the first time on 21 January 1837. The old workhouse near Town's Moor dated from 1764, but by the mid-nineteenth century could no longer meet Blackburn's demands. The New Union Workhouse, pictured here, was constructed on a thirty-acre site on a hill to the south-east of the town centre, at a cost of £30,000. It opened on 2 April 1864 and was designed to hold 700 inmates. It was deliberately built in such a prominent situation to serve as a continuing reminder to Blackburn's population of the consequences of failing to work hard. It is now part of Queen's Park Hospital but remains an imposing feature, looking out over the town.

The Hindle residence, King Street, 1955. This mansion was originally built by John and Elizabeth Hindle in 1773 and had an arched entrance into a courtyard at the rear. In 1824 it was the the home of John Fowden Hindle who later bought Woodfold Hall. The mansion was later converted into shops, one of which became the town's post office where Thomas Butterworth was postmaster. The courtyard gave access to the Old Borough Police Office, a converted warehouse in Clayton Street.

The Friends' Meeting House was built in the early nineteenth century on Paradise Terrace. It is still there, hidden among the small businesses that have sprung up in that area, and remains a simple but very attractive building.

St Paul's was built in 1791 but the vicar of Blackburn would not certify it for consecration. It was not until 1829 that the church was eventually consecrated and the minister, Reverend John Price, admitted to the Church of England. This photograph was taken in 1950, six years before it was demolished.

When this photograph was taken in the 1880s, St Mary's was still the local parish church. Designed by John Palmer, its construction was begun in the 1820s when it replaced a church which dated back to the reign of Henry VIII. This impressive structure was always viewed as the main place of worship in the town and when the new Blackburn diocese was formed in 1926, it was an automatic choice to become Blackburn Cathedral.

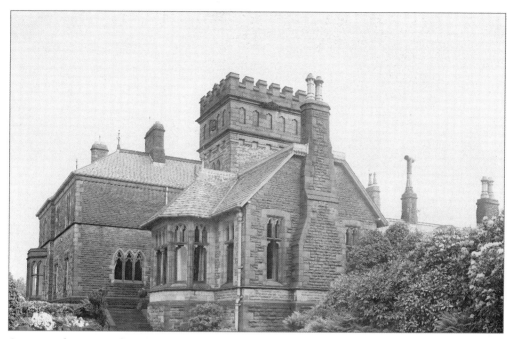

Quarry Bank House, a fine stone building with a small tower, stood on Billinge Hill surrounded by four acres of land. In 1926 it was chosen to be the official residence of the new Bishop of Blackburn.

Little Harwood Conservative Club was opened by the local MP Mr Hornby in April 1894. It was formerly the home of the Claytons and was converted at a cost of £266. Facilities included a reading room, card room, billiard table and a large bowling green. The De Clayton family had been granted the manor lands of Little Harwood in the thirteenth century and were associated with Blackburn's affairs for several hundred years. In the early nineteenth century, Thomas Clayton sold off the estate in a number of lots; the family home was also sold.

Built in 1883, Thwaites Arcade linked Church Street to Lord Street. It provided Blackburn's more affluent shoppers with an elegant covered shopping area. It was eventually demolished in 1971.

The co-operative movement flourished in the town and in 1920, the Blackburn (Amalgamated) Co-operative Society was formed. This photograph was taken in 1930 when the Emporium opened on Town Hall Street. In the 1970s it became the town's main library.

Only the best and most modern was good enough for the Emporium and here, staff are registering the cash with the most up-to-date technology.

The first floor of the Emporium was given over almost exclusively to women. There was a millinery department and a section in which furs were sold. This delightful photograph shows the corsetry area.

Blackburn's traditional indoor market was a popular and busy shopping area. This 1952 photograph conveys something of the hustle and bustle of the place.

On 30 November 1891 a gas explosion ripped through the Crown Hotel and Sixpenny Bazaar on Victoria Street, killing five people. It took the fire brigade four hours to dig out the landlord, Mr Houghton, who had to be continuously hosed with water to prevent him from being burnt to death.

In May 1878 the mill operatives of East Lancashire were embroiled in a bitter industrial dispute with their employers. Blackburn suffered greatly and on the evening of 15 May a crowd visited the home of Mr Fish, an employer, to demand food. He gave the mob some provisions but they still broke his windows and threatened to burn down his house. They attacked the home of a grocer and then went to the Oddfellows Arms on King Street to demand liquor. The landlord, Mr Rogerson, agreed to their demands but still had vitriol thrown into his face, which blinded him.

On 11 May, protestors became angry when they heard that negotiations to settle the dispute had broken down. They therefore attacked the home of the employers' chief negotiator, Colonel Robert Raynsford Jackson. This was Clayton Manor in Wilpshire, which is seen here the morning after the mob had broken into the house and used two cans of paraffin oil they found there to set light to it. The house was gutted and such was the ferocity of the blaze it could be seen from fifteen miles away. The dispute had arisen when the mill owners had decided to cut wages by 10 per cent, but despite the widespread rioting, the workers were defeated and returned to work the following month.

On 1 February 1824 the Dispensary at 56 King Street, seen here in 1952, was opened. In its first year 1,513 patients were treated and although it was soon realized that a larger infirmary was needed, it served Blackburn well for another fifteen years.

By the middle of the century the need for a new infirmary was a priority, and in a competition seventy-three architects submitted plans. The winner was James Turnbull, and on an eight-acre site purchased from the Fielden family, the Blackburn and East Lancashire Infirmary opened in 1863.

The Palace was originally built in 1899 as a theatre, which closed down in 1932. Four years later it reopened as a cinema and remained so until 1957. Three years later it again opened as a cinema, only to be converted into a bingo hall in 1964, pictured here in 1966. In 1975 it was converted yet again to a cinema before finally closing in 1984, after which it was demolished. In all these various capacities the Palace thus played an important part in the leisure activities of many generations of Blackburn folk.

This 1935 photograph shows the Savoy cinema, decorated for that year's Silver Jubilee celebrations. It opened in 1922 and was the first cinema in Blackburn to show a 'talkie' in 1929. Originally owned by the Yorke family, it was leased to ABC and closed in 1957.

There was some controversy when Belper Street Baths opened in 1906 and mixed bathing was allowed. There were strict rules governing costumes and men had to be accompanied by at least one female. Nevertheless, as many as 200 bathers attended these pioneering swimming sessions.

BLACKBURN AT WORK

Industrial disputes were inevitable in factories, and this photograph shows striking mill workers in the Nab Lane area in the 1920s.

The grocery staff at the Daiseyfield Co-operative Society branch at 445 Whalley New Road pose proudly outside their store in the 1890s. This was one of the branches that merged to create the Blackburn (Amalgamated) Co-operative Society in 1920.

Clogs had always been important to mill workers and they relied heavily on local firms to produce them. One of these was J. Fowler's Boot and Clog Warehouse at the corner of Whalley New Road and Plane Street – the staff stand smartly outside the premises.

Blackburn's original fire station was situated in the appropriately named and long since disappeared Engine Street. In 1867 a new station was founded in Clayton Street, where this group photograph was taken in the 1890s.

One of the horse-drawn engines used by the brigade in 1905.

Volunteer firemen were used until 1882, when the local brigade was reorganized and became the responsibility of the chief constable. Therefore it is not surprising to find a police officer posing on the left of this group, out on a practice with a steam engine in about 1910.

This photograph was taken in the 1920s, by which time the brigade had moved from Clayton Street into new premises at Byrom Street.

Members of Blackburn fire brigade are seen here taking part in a training exercise on Northgate in the early 1900s.

The old Blackburn gasworks, established in 1818, came under the corporation's control in 1877. There were gasworks at Greenbank and in Addison Street, an office in Jubilee Street and gasholders in Addison Street and Grimshaw Park Road. In this early twentieth-century photograph, the labourers in the retort room of the Greenbank works briefly pose for the camera.

This is the workforce of Fielding & McCarthy, a firm of decorators, with their handcart outside their Cleaver Street premises in 1904. George Fielding and William McCarthy were the owners.

Coal was taken from the Lower Darwen Colliery to Shadsworth Road, where it was converted into coke. This was the last mine to be worked in the Blackburn area and it closed in 1917.

Coal merchants Crook & Thompson, established in 1847, had used horses to make deliveries for many years and in 1920 were still using thirty-six animals. By the time this photograph was taken in 1936, the company was using motor vehicles more widely but still used horses for short distances and light loads.

The process by which matted cotton was transformed into a finished fabric involved several stages. These carding machines in Higher Audley Street Mill, seen here in 1941, cleaned and separated the cotton fibres.

These ring spinning machines, also at the Higher Audley Street Mill, twisted the cotton fibres on to spools.

This scene shows the winding process at Alma Street Mill in 1950.

It was on looms such as these, at the Britannia Mill in 1940, that the fabric was produced.

Although pictured in 1966, this view of
Hornby Mill on Enamel Street gives some idea
of how the town must have looked when
cotton dominated the economy of Blackburn.
The channel running down the centre of the
picture took waste water down to the river.

The manager, in his suit, poses with the tacklers in their fustian waistcoats at Roe Lee Mill in about 1900.
A tackler looked after the looms and had an undeserved reputation for stupidity and laziness. Many
apocryphal stories were told about them and 'tacklers tales' were a source of widespread amusement in
Blackburn and other cotton towns.

A weaving shed at Britannia Mill in the early 1920s. Rose Spei, on the left, and her workmate Teresa Turner pause to have this evocative photograph taken. In their belts they carry all the necessary tools for making running repairs.

Rowland Baguley and Co. were shuttle manufacturers who moved to Blackburn from Manchester in the 1850s, when the founder recognized the growing importance of the town to the cotton industry. This Edwardian scene of their Addison Street foundry shows the forge and smithy. At this time 5,000 shuttles were produced weekly.

More than fifty men and boys were employed by Rowland Baguley and Co. and this photograph shows some of those responsible for polishing and grinding.

The British Northop Loom Company, founded in 1902, owed its rapid growth to the manufacture of the automatic loom. This photograph of James Gavigan was taken in June 1955, in the research department of the Philips Road factory.

This photograph, also taken in June 1955, shows members of the company's research department. From left to right on the back row: Fred Foy, Fred Hunter and James Gavigan. Seated are R. Dinsdale and Fred Smith.

This scene shows British Northop's automatic looms in operation in the Alma Street Mill, 1950.

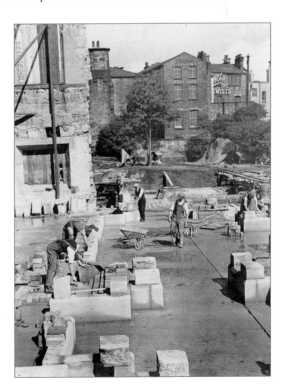

Bricklayers hard at work in 1937 on the extension
to Blackburn Cathedral.

Appleby's Flour Mill was an important employer in the town and this steam engine, photographed in the 1960s, performed valuable service in the firm's depot.

In this late Victorian scene, the ferryman at Hacking helps passengers to disembark.

PUBS & BREWERIES

The Old Bull Hotel was one of Blackburn's most famous hostelries and in the early nineteenth century mail coaches departed from it daily for many different parts of the country. In the 1890s proprietor Mrs Mitchell promoted it as both a commercial and family hotel – guests were met at the railway station in the hotel's own carriage. When it was demolished after the Second World War, a major part of the town's history disappeared.

This 1890 photograph of Dutton's Brewery shows the drays that were used then, together with the wooden barrels. The company was founded by Thomas Dutton and his son William in the late eighteenth century. In 1807 they began to acquire tied houses in Blackburn and among their first pubs were the Golden Ball, Hare and Hounds and the Lord Nelson. By the end of the nineteenth century the Dutton family ties ended and the brewery eventually merged with Whitbread in 1964.

The Golden Lion on Church Street was a well-known Dutton's pub from which wagons ran a delivery service to Burnley twice a week in the 1820s.

Originally the Galligreaves Hotel was a private residence, the last owner being blacksmith Joseph Harrison. On his death in 1880, Dutton's took it over but its semicircular entrance porch with steps and pillars was typical of a private Georgian mansion.

The Lord Nelson on Penney Street was one of the earliest pubs to be a Dutton's tied house.

Blackburn's breweries depended upon horse-drawn drays for many years and here draymen from Thwaites' Brewery make their deliveries in the traditional manner. Established in 1807, the company has remained in the town ever since and its modern premises dominate the town's skyline.

The Livesey New Inn on Livesey Branch Road, *c.* 1930. This was one of Thwaites' most popular pubs, with its bowling green proving to be an added attraction.

The Bay Horse at Salford figured in the town's affairs for many years. Dating from the eighteenth century it was one of the oldest coaching inns, and in its courtyard which adjoined the Blackburn Mail Office, the teams of post horses were tended to.

The Duke of York on Darwen Street was built in about 1790 and named after George III's son. When this 1954 photograph was taken it still retained many of its original features. For instance an old stone mounting block, used by farmer's wives riding pillion, was still in its existing position.

The King's Head on the corner of King Street and Freckleton Street was built in 1765. At that time, it was visited regularly by the bleachers who came to Blackburn to collect calico pieces from the various warehouses in the vicinity.

St Johns Tavern on Ainsworth Street was important in the town's social life. In the early 1800s the Company of Archers had their annual dinner there, and during one social function a sedan chair was reported stolen from outside its door.

The Castle Hotel on Market Street Lane belonged to the Lion Brewery and was especially striking. Its major features were two semicircular bays, three storeys high, which were crowned by battlements.

The Lion Brewery was owned by Nuttalls until the 1920s when it was taken over by Matthew Brown's of Preston, who subsequently decided to expand in Blackburn. In this 1951 photograph one of the brewery's delivery vans, decorated for the centenary celebrations, is parked outside the Lion Brewery.

GETTING AROUND

In the eighteenth century attempts were made to fund road building by introducing tolls. In 1819 a road between Langho and Brookhouse was opened, and a toll bar erected where the new road branched off from Whalley Old Road. This Brookhouse scene shows where the toll bar stood before its removal. This entire area was redeveloped in 1928.

In 1824 Henry Austin began a passenger service on the canal between Blackburn and Burnley. This delightful rounded building was his headquarters. Two horses pulled the boats which were fitted with saloon cabins – the journey lasted four hours in all.

This photograph of Nova Scotia Locks highlights the massive scale of industrial development along the Leeds and Liverpool Canal in the first half of the nineteenth century. From left to right, the chimneys belong to Victoria Mill, Highfield Mill, Albert Mill, Infirmary Mill and Atlantic Mill.

With the transporting of goods made that much easier, James Rodgett's Canal Mill at Eanam was one of more than thirty built along the canal. Built in 1824 it was, by the time this view was taken a century later, a storehouse for a local foundry.

One of the other mills constructed on the canal was Wharf Street Mill, seen here from the towpath.

T. and J. Hodson was a long-established boat builders whose boatyard was on the canal at Whitebirk. There is something rather sad about this photograph; it shows the last boat ever to be built at the yard.

This is the yard in happier times with some of the workforce standing by the barge *Alice*, which was being built for Tomlinsons, the coal carriers.

This 1946 photograph shows the launch of the barge *Peter*, in the traditional manner, at the Whitebirk yard. Vessels were launched sideways down the slipway and the effect could be very dramatic.

Coal was crucial to Blackburn's growth and Crook & Thompson played an integral role in this business. They were the town's leading coal merchants and this view from the 1930s shows their wharf at Audley Bridge.

Built in 1875 at Feniscowles, Star Paper Mills produced 200 tons of paper each week. The eight huge boilers needed 400 tons of coal weekly; this was carried on a tramway operated by a rotating cable from the canal.

Some of the sixty recruits to the Girls' Canal Barge Service, formed because of manpower shortages during the Second World War, are given a demonstration in knot tying at Whitebirk.

This photograph, taken on 24 August 1867, shows the civil engineering works in the Roddlesworth Valley during the construction of the Blackburn to Chorley railway. Earlier in the century, the Leeds–Liverpool Canal had a significant impact on the economic development of the town and the railways added further impetus to its growth in the middle of the century. The line between Blackburn and Preston opened in 1846 and extensions were added in subsequent years, including a line between Blackburn and Accrington in 1848. In 1864 a company was formed to build a new line from Blackburn to Chorley, Wigan and St Helens, to join with the Manchester and Liverpool Railway at Huyton. This network of lines was completed in 1869, thus linking Liverpool and the cotton towns of East Lancashire.

Blackburn railway station, photographed in 1905, was a splendid Victorian construction and demonstrated the importance of the town as the railways expanded during the century.

As the canal's economic significance lessened, its importance in recreational terms grew. Between 5 and 10 August 1965, the Inland Waterways Association National Boat Rally took place. In this view the mayor, Councillor Laurence Edwards, reviews the participating boats.

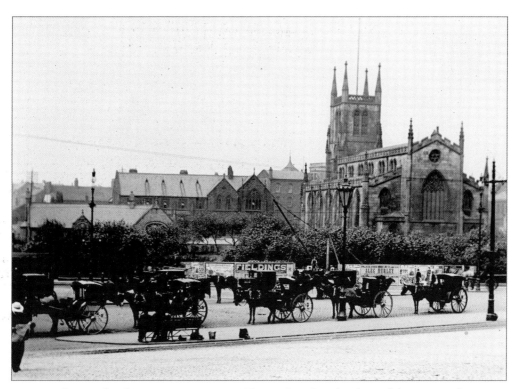

Hansom cabs wait for their next passengers on The Boulevard at the close of the nineteenth century. Tranquil scenes such as this were not to last much longer.

The motor car's potential had been recognized by some individuals and by 1913 the town had two car body-building firms and two garages. This photograph, taken in about 1910, shows one of Blackburn's three motor engineers, Thomas Burton of New Park Street, in a car designed and built by himself.

The Boulevard again in the 1920s and the revolutionary developments in transport are clear. Gone are the hansoms and in their place is a Leyland single-decker, a charabanc and several cars, including a bull-nose Morris.

An early steam tram at the cemetery gates, *c.* 1890. The smaller engine pulled the tram and was fitted with a small boiler. Large amounts of smoke and sparks came out of its long chimney, from which the passengers were protected by a roof on the tram itself.

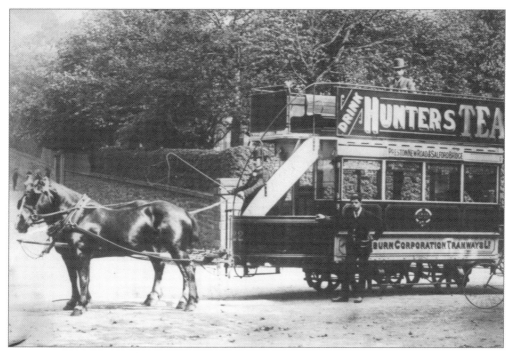

Horse-drawn trams were introduced on the Preston New Road route in 1888; one of them is seen here. An extra horse was required on this route to provide additional 'pull', up Montague Street.

The phasing out of Blackburn's trams was postponed owing to the Second World War. This photograph of number 58 on the Wilpshire route shows the front light prepared for the blackout. During the war 15 million passengers were carried annually.

By 1903 the entire system had been electrified and trams were normally open-topped such as number 66, photographed here at the Church terminus. A decision to cover all of the trams was abandoned when it was later decided to replace them with buses.

The Boulevard in the 1920s shows trams and taxis competing for passengers.

Thousands of people lined the streets to see Blackburn's last tram make its way to the Intack depot on 3 September 1949. Decorated with bunting, it was driven by the chairman of the Transport Department, Bob Weir, who was assisted by veteran driver, Mr W. Dyball.

The massive increase in motor traffic meant that specialized policing was needed. This is the Motor Patrol of the Blackburn force, set up as a result of the 1930 Road Traffic Act.

Holme Street in the 1950s, with two buses at the Wilpshire terminus to the right. On the left, waiting at the crossing, is a newer Crossley-bodied double-decker which had been introduced in 1947.

A Leyland double-decker runs on the Mill Hill route in the mid-1960s. This was one of eight older buses given new bodywork by a local company, Lancashire Coachwork Builders, between 1954 and 1956.

This double-decker entered service on 1 March 1938 but was not selected to have new bodywork. It was sold for scrap in July 1957.

This single-decker is parked at the old bus stop on Northgate in the mid-1960s, and is about to set off on the West Park Road route. This particular vehicle entered service on 26 March 1948 and was withdrawn on 31 March 1967.

Blackburn's buses were introduced on 1 November 1929 and by the time this photograph was taken at the railway station terminus in the 1950s, 43 million fare-paying passengers were being carried annually.

Truly the end of an era as enthusiasts and locals say farewell to steam. Pacific Steam Locomotive *Oliver Cromwell* leaves Blackburn station for the last time in April 1968.

EDUCATION

Blackburn's grammar school opened in the early sixteenth century, and in 1567 Queen Elizabeth I granted it a charter which led to the adoption of the name Queen Elizabeth Grammar School. It has occupied many sites in the town and this 1870 photograph is of the relatively small premises in Freckleton Street, from where it moved in 1886.

The Girls' Charity School in Thunder Alley opened in 1764 to teach pauper girls reading, knitting, sewing and spinning. It closed in January 1884 and was used as commercial premises until it was demolished in July 1928.

The Independent Academy in Ainsworth Street opened in 1816 to educate students for the Independent Ministry. The Academy moved to a site in Manchester in 1840 and when this photograph was taken in 1957, a firm of solicitors was occupying the building.

All Saints Ragged School, Russell Street, is seen here in the early twentieth century. These schools began in the 1840s and catered for the very poorest children, usually ragged in appearance, whose parents could not afford even the lowest fees of other schools. They were much criticized but provided shelter and compassion for the most vulnerable of children.

The Blackburn Ragged School Prize Band in 1896.

The pupils and mistress of St Paul's School pose for this photograph taken in the 1880s. By this time education was available for all, but local schools still aimed essentially to provide mill workers for the nearby industries – particularly from among the girls.

This 1892 photograph was taken at Witton School which maintained strong links with the Fielden family. For instance in February 1854, Lieutenant General Fielden provided breakfast for all those pupils whose parents were out of work.

Form 1B of the Church of England Central School pose with their master for this photograph in 1921. The church had been particularly important in the development of education in Victorian Blackburn where, unfortunately, the authorities had given it little priority.

Pupils and teacher of St Joseph's School in 1911.

This late Victorian view shows Ewood Board School which was one of three such establishments built in Blackburn under the terms of the 1870 Education Act. These were for youngsters who could not be accommodated in existing schools.

A little girl peeps out from behind a postbox at the impressive Technical College. The Prince of Wales laid the foundation stone in May 1888 and the vocational education it provided in building, engineering and textiles made it popular with Blackburn's employers.

The reading room in Blackburn Library in the 1920s. Public libraries had been established in 1850 and aimed to provide even the poorest individuals with the means of improving their minds, through access to books and newspapers.

Children were also encouraged to use libraries and this is the children's section in 1926. One wonders how long it took the photographer to get them to pose so studiously for the camera.

Roe Lee Council Junior School opened on 11 July 1929 and was the first new school to be built in Blackburn for almost twenty years. The emphasis now was on creating a spacious, light and airy environment in which children could be encouraged to learn.

This is the assembly hall at Roe Lee Council Junior School when it first opened.

SECTION SEVEN

A TOWN AT WAR

Entertainers were often used to boost morale during the Second World War and George Formby visited Blackburn on 4 February 1942, to help the campaign to save waste paper. He arrived at the town hall in a Ministry of Information loudspeaker van, from which he entertained a large crowd. He is seen here with his wife and local leaders, signing the visitors' book in the town hall.

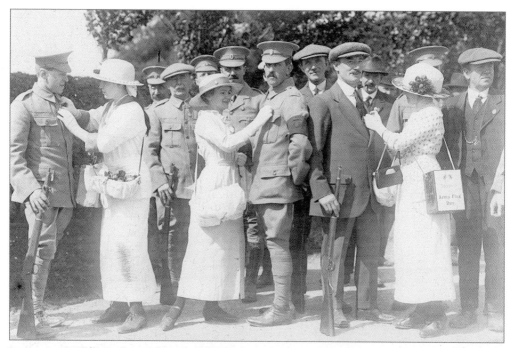

In August 1915 the Preston Volunteer Defence Corps held a camp at Witton Park. They stayed several days and staged an athletics meeting on one of the days. In this poignant photograph, volunteers and possible recruits are encouraged by some of Blackburn's young women to help raise funds.

Volunteers parade at Witton Park Drill Hall in August 1915. It would no doubt be a sad task to try and discover how many of these proud men survived the war.

The mayor, Alderman Laurence Cotton, stands on a tank in front of the Sessions House on Northgate, during a savings drive for the war effort in February 1918.

As a mark of respect to those citizens of Blackburn who were lost in the First World War, this beautiful garden of remembrance was laid out in Corporation Park. It opened, without a ceremony, on 10 July 1923.

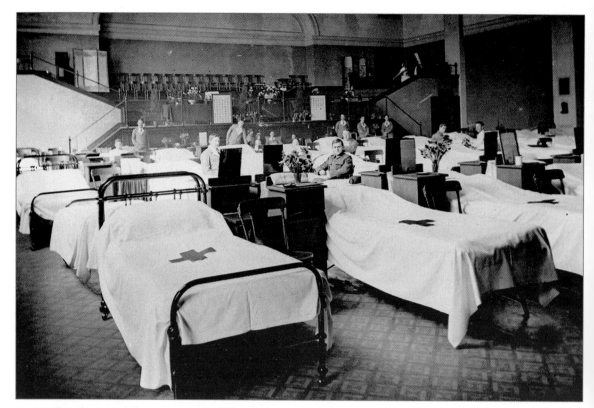

This photograph from the First World War shows some of the wounded in the Public Halls, which had been converted into a military hospital. Given the large number of wounded men, the normal hospital service could not cope and various buildings were put under the auspices of the Red Cross and adapted to meet these new demands. In Blackburn, Blakey Moor Council School was one of the first to be so used and was followed by a number of private residences. These included those of Captain Fielden in Witton Park, John Duckworth's The Knolle and Ellerslie, the home of J.G. Ramsbottom which overlooked Corporation Park. In May 1917, the Corporation placed the Public Halls at the disposal of the War Hospital Committee. It cost 1s 6d each day to feed a patient and the people of Blackburn donated money, tobacco, cigarettes, flowers and newspapers, together with a piano and billiard tables. Within a few months, a total of 732 wounded troops from this country, Australia, Canada, New Zealand and Belgium were treated there. Of these, 456 were discharged for duty, 18 had been invalided out of the services, 155 had been transferred to other hospitals and 103 remained in the Public Halls.

In this photograph taken in December 1939, Alderman Hamer, in the centre of the front row with Chief Constable Looms on his right, and Superintendent Langley to his left, sit with those Blackburn police officers who had been recalled to the colours.

Throughout the Second World War, Blackburn's Auxiliary Fire Service played an integral part in protecting life and property. In this wartime photograph, members of the service take a break from training in the Billinge Road area.

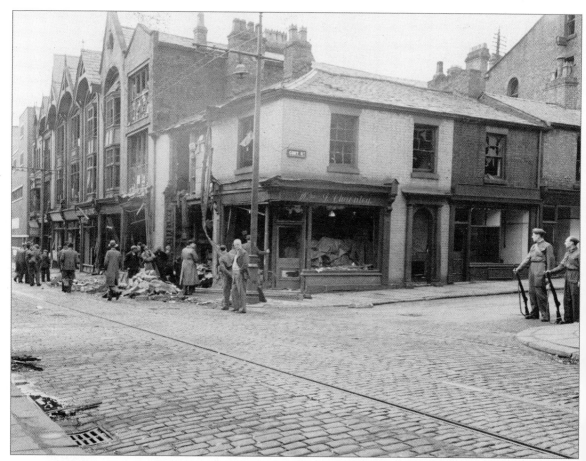

Blackburn suffered relatively little damage from bombing raids during the Second World War. However, just before noon on 31 August 1940, a bomb weighing approximately 200 kilograms fell on Ainsworth Street. The extent of the damage can be gauged from this photograph taken shortly afterwards.

In April 1943, Blackburn's Wings for Victory Week raised an incredible £1,213,008 for the construction of fifty aircraft. The week began with an impressive parade, and in this photograph members of the Home Guard march along Darwen Street.

With the cessation of the European war on 8 May 1945, many street parties were held throughout the town. On a more formal level, church services were held the following Sunday, succeeded by a Victory Parade, part of which is pictured here.

Wartime Britain witnessed the setting up of British Restaurants and this 1942 photograph is of the Blackburn area's first, in Mayson Street. The idea behind them was to provide communal meals, meaning the nation's supplies were spread more widely, while at the same time providing consumers with good wholesome meals more cheaply than they could make them at home. It was intended that workers would have at least one meal each day and the restaurants were aimed mainly at adults – it was hoped children would be sufficiently catered for at school.

This is the rather austere and functional dining room of the Mayson Street British Restaurant. Hundreds ate there daily, and when this photograph was taken in February 1942 the most popular food was Swiss roll.

This is an interior view of the 'Pyramid' air raid shelter, manufactured by the local engineering company of Foster, Yates and Thom Ltd during the Second World War.

The Home Guard performed many important tasks during the war and in this photograph, taken in late 1941, members of No. 1 Platoon of the 10th Lancashire Battalion are on manoeuvres near New Inns.

Two months after No. 1 Platoon was photographed in October 1944, the Home Guard was stood down. When this happened and after a civic luncheon, the original commanding officer, Colonel R.F. Mottershead, took the salute at a march past of some of the 7,000 local men who had served in the 10th Battalion during the war.

SECTION EIGHT

HIGH DAYS & HOLIDAYS

These are some of the 160 guests who attended the fiftieth anniversary dinner of the forming of Blackburn Rovers, at the Furness Café on 8 December 1925.

One of Blackburn's single-decker trams decorated for the coronation of King George V in 1911.

Blackburn's firemen welcomed the Prince and Princess of Wales with this arch on Preston New Road on 9 May 1888. It was formed by two extended ladders joined at the top by a wooden circular bridge and it rose thirty-five feet above the road.

On 10 July 1913, King George V and Queen Mary visited Blackburn to lay the foundation stone of the Public Halls. They also visited Roe Lee Mill, where the Queen is greeted by John Duckworth, co-owner of the mill.

Queen Elizabeth II is photographed visiting Mullards, a local electrical engineering company, in April 1955. She is with Mr C. de Wit, one of the firm's directors.

The foundation stone of the infirmary's new Victoria Wing – so named to commemorate Queen Victoria's sixty years' reign – is laid by the mayor, Frederick Baynes on 21 June 1897. A sealed jar was buried with it containing a commemorative medal, copies of local newspapers and the infirmary's latest annual report.

The driver of this cart, which is decorated by the Horticultural Society for a pageant in 1902, is Mr A. Bulmer. He is accompanied by Alfred Nuttall, the society's president for that year.

Before the introduction of state pensions, the elderly relied to some extent on charity. Here, Blackburn's senior citizens sit down to a meal paid for by the Mayor's Fund, on 3 March 1906.

Mayor's Sunday on 12 November 1905. Traditionally the newly elected mayor, in this case Mr F.T. Thomas, led local organizations and public officials from the town hall to the parish church; this was witnessed by thousands of spectators.

This tram has been specially decorated for Blackburn's Shopping Week in October 1921. Organized by the local Chamber of Trade, a quarter of a million shoppers were attracted to the town.

In 1951 Blackburn celebrated the centenary of its charter being granted. The whole town became involved and this is the Information Bureau, where tickets for all of the events could be obtained.

The custom of perambulating the parish boundary was widespread until the nineteenth century. In the days before maps were widely used, it enabled details of the parish boundary to be passed from generation to generation. No obstacle was too great and many a young boy was dragged though a bog, or made to climb over a house if the boundary ran through it. This photograph, taken on 11 August 1951, shows members of Blackburn Ramblers' Association reviving the custom as part of the town's centenary celebrations, and crossing the canal at Whitebirk in a rowing-boat.

This splendid group of Blackburn Conservatives picnicked at Bolton Woods in 1898.

Children from Holy Souls Catholic Church prepare for the May custom of 'Crowning Our Lady', in the early 1950s. The young girl at the rear is carrying the crown on a cushion.

Although no longer widely observed, annual works' outings were popular right up until the outbreak of the Second World War. This group was snapped at Blackburn railway station in the summer of 1934, waiting to go to Fountains Abbey. Some of those posing may have been from other companies but most were on the staff of William Tattersall and Sons Ltd, wholesale provision merchants of King William Street.

CANON SINKER ADMITS DR HERBERT
TO THE CATHEDRAL, BLACKBURN. 28.2.27.

With the creation of the new Blackburn diocese, the confirmation of the first bishop, the Right Reverend Percy Mark Herbert, took place at York Minster on 26 January 1927. One month later, on 28 February, he was enthroned at Blackburn's new cathedral. While the Bishop of Manchester bade farewell to those leaving his diocese, Bishop Herbert knocked on the West door. This contemporary postcard shows Canon Sinker, the vicar of Blackburn, opening the door, whereupon the new bishop was enthroned.

In this photograph, taken on 1 November 1956, the mayor, Mr W. Henshall, is shown buying the first premium bond in Blackburn.

It is obviously a red-letter day for local girl Teresa Higginson, aged five years. She is posing for the camera in 1908, having just received this new dress and doll from relatives in America.

Blackburn's traditional Easter Fair had been held in the market-place since 1852. By then it had become a pleasure fair as its significance as a trading centre had greatly diminished. In Victorian times there were stalls for gingerbread, brandy snaps, ginger beer, black puddings and other delicacies. In the sideshows it was possible to see the 'female giantess', conjurors and Chinese fireworks. This photograph, taken in 1964, is of the last Easter Fair to be held in the market-place, just before it was redeveloped. By then it was a typical modern fair with a flying coaster and big wheel.

SOME BLACKBURN FOLK

The Blackburn Subscription Bowling Club photographed at their annual competition in the 1890s. The club existed as long ago as 1734 and their original green was at the foot of the slope of Cicely Hole.

The committee, members and friends of the Blackburn and District Horticultural Society enjoy a trip to Lathom Hall, Ormskirk in 1905.

Brass bands have long been a feature of life in the north of England – this is the Blackburn Public Brass Band in 1905.

In 1874 a group of local enthusiasts formed a football club which eventually took the name Blackburn Rovers. In 1888 the club was one of the founding members of the Football League but by then the club had already established a formidable reputation as cup fighters. It was their rivals, Blackburn Olympic, who in 1883 became the first northern team to win the FA Cup, although Rovers had been the losing finalists the previous year and went on to win the cup five times between 1884 and 1891. This is the team which lost the 1882 final against Old Etonians at The Oval. Back row, left to right: L. Greenwood (did not play in the final), R. Howarth, J. Hargreaves, F. Suter, W. Duckworth (umpire). Middle row: J. Duckworth, H. McIntyre, H. Sharples, F.W. Hargreaves, T. Strachan, G. Avery. Front row: J. Brown, J. Douglas.

In 1928 Rovers won the cup again at Wembley, beating the mighty Huddersfield Town by three goals to one. This is the victorious side together with club officials, posing with the trophy.

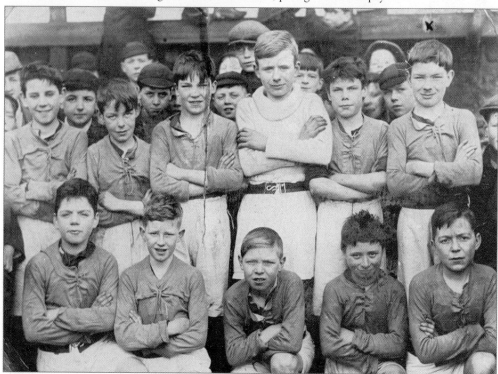

Schoolboy soccer has always been popular in the town. On 23 January 1932 in the final of the Blackburn Schoolboys' Football Association Cup, Mill Hill St Peter's beat Emanuel Church of England School by one goal to nil, and this is the victorious team.

Ever since the earliest days of a professional police force in the nineteenth century, the part played by sport in building self-confidence, strength and team work has always been recognized. Traditionally, therefore, the police have participated in many sports – this is the Blackburn Borough Police tug of war team in 1901.

Blackburn police also formed a popular swimming club, members of which pose in this early twentieth-century photograph.

Officers at the Duckworth Street police station pose shortly before the First World War. At this time the main police office was on King Street, with other stations at Copy Nook and Russell Street.

Blackburn's detectives pose in their formal dress worn for an inspection in the 1920s. On the back row, from left to right, are Detectives Shimmin, McCartney and Nolan; on the front row, Detectives Winstanley, Kenyon and Cooper.

Sergeant William Fielding was one of the town's earliest policemen. He is seen here in the 1860s.

This, believe it or not, is a Christmas card, sent jointly in 1929 from the House of Commons by the town's two MPs, Harry Gill and Mary Hamilton. The reverse is slightly more seasonal and carries a festive message.

Eli Pickup of 45 Thomas Street — originally built by his grandfather — was the third generation of the family to live in the house. The Pickups were coal dealers and Eli died on 22 June 1926, aged eighty-nine years.

Mr and Mrs Alfred Woods had been married for fifty-seven years when this picture was taken in 1957. They were retired weavers, aged eighty-four and eighty-two years respectively, having started work when they were both ten years old. Alfred retired aged seventy-two, and his wife aged sixty-four.

The full splendour of the mayor's robes is evident in this studio portrait of Councillor Robert Parkinson, Blackburn's mayor from 1875 to 1876.

The town's leading photographer and postcard publisher of his time was A.E. Shaw, seen here in 1910. He sold views of local buildings, people and disasters. Presumably the bicycle was useful for getting about the district.

This staff group from Blackburn Public Library dates from 1900. The librarians, Mr Pomfrit and Mr Ashton, are on the right-hand side of the back row.

This photograph taken in November 1933 of a scene from *The Old Order and The New* shows Kathleen Ferrier, world-famous contralto, who grew up in Blackburn. She is seated on the left and is sporting a moustache. She died of cancer at the zenith of her fame on 8 October 1953.

The Public Halls were opened by Lord Derby on 21 October 1921. He is pictured here in the top hat on the front row, along with a number of Blackburn's dignitaries.

It is 1926, two decades before the creation of the National Health Service, and the Guardians' Infirmary Committee visits Queen's Park Hospital for the opening of a new nurses' home.

As the fire brigade expanded and was modernized, it was necessary to move from the old Clayton Street headquarters. Premises were found in Byrom Street which were officially opened on 18 May 1922. Besides fire-fighting equipment, space was also provided for ambulances and stables for the police horses. This is the official opening party. Back row, left to right: W.H. Dent (contractor), Walter Stirrup (architect), Councillor W.H. Grimshaw, Councillor D.E. Brierley. Front row: C. Hodson (Chief Constable), Alderman James Kay, Alderman J. Fielding (Mayor), Sir Lewis Beard (Town Clerk) and Councillor E. Hamer.

A few days before the end of the war in May 1945, the local Labour Party nominated Lewis John Edwards and Barbara Castle as the candidates for the forthcoming general election. Of the five people interviewed, he received sixty-three votes, and she fifty-three. She was thirty-three years old and had already enjoyed academic success at Oxford University and as a journalist. In 1937 she became the youngest member of St Pancras Borough Council. Her first public appearance in Blackburn was at the Public Halls on 17 May 1945, which was to be the beginning of a life-long association with the town.

   This is one of the earliest photographs taken of her campaigning in 1945. Elected on 5 July 1945, she remained the town's MP until 1979, having enjoyed a successful career as a leading politician. She became a Member of the European Parliament and entered the House of Lords in 1990, taking the name the Rt. Hon. Baroness of Blackburn.

ACKNOWLEDGEMENTS

Many people assisted in the compilation of this book and I would especially wish to thank the following for permission to use photographs and other assistance: the staff of Blackburn Library, particularly Ian Sutton and Bhawna Patel; Lancashire Constabulary; *Lancashire Evening Telegraph*; Terry Gavigan and Celia Smith. At home, I had the support of Philip, Rachel and Claire.

BRITAIN IN OLD PHOTOGRAPHS